T.J. SMITH

Jesus: God With Us - Christmas Devotional

First edition

This book was professionally typeset on Reedsy.
Find out more at reedsy.com

Contents

Introduction

Every December, we step into a season filled with light, memories, and anticipation. But beneath all of it is a truth so staggering it still reshapes lives thousands of years later: **The God who created everything didn't stay distant. He stepped into our story.**

Christmas announces that the infinite became an infant, the Creator entered creation, and the Holy One walked into the world not with shock and awe but with humility and mercy. He didn't send help from a distance. He drew close enough to touch, close enough to weep, close enough to save.

This devotional is an invitation to slow down long enough to remember that. To re-enter the wonder. To see again that the heart of Christmas is not sentiment — it's the nearness of God.

Throughout these 25 days, you'll hear from different voices within our Parkway Church family — Senior Pastor **Greg Morris**, Pastor **William (Bill) Reid**, Pastor **Aaron Routon**, and Pastor **T.J. Smith**. Each brings a unique perspective, a different style, a different way of pointing toward the same Savior.

Allow each day's reflection to meet you where you are. Let Scripture steady your mind. Let Christ settle your heart. Because if God is truly with us, then none of us walk into this season alone. Even the places that feel heavy, complicated, or unfinished are not abandoned. They are held by the One who came near.

May these 25 days draw you deeper into that reality and awaken a fresh sense of wonder, worship, and hope.

December 1 – Angel to Zechariah

by Pastor Greg Morris

"But the angel said to him, 'Do not be afraid, Zechariah, because your prayer has been heard. Your wife Elizabeth will bear you a son, and you will name him John.'" – Luke 1:13

"God's promises are like the stars; the darker the night, the brighter they shine." – David Nicholas

Reflection:

The incense smoke curled upward in the Holy Place, carrying the prayers of Israel toward heaven. Zechariah's hands trembled—not from age, though he was well past his prime—but from the profound honor of this moment. Once in a lifetime, perhaps never, a priest might be chosen by lot to burn incense in the temple. After decades of faithful service, today was his day. Then everything changed. To the right of the altar stood a figure blazing with otherworldly light.

"Do not be afraid, Zechariah; your prayer has been heard. Your wife Elizabeth will bear you a son, and you are to call him John."

After decades of whispered pity, after years of accepted barrenness, after hope had long since died… a son? "How can I be sure of this?" The words escaped before wisdom could catch them.

Gabriel's response blazed with holy authority: "I stand in the presence of God." And because Zechariah had asked for proof, he would get it. Nine months of silence. Nine months to ponder whether God needed his belief to accomplish the impossible.

Have you ever stood at the intersection of God's promise and your doubt? Zechariah had prayed for a child for years—perhaps decades. But when the answer finally came, it seemed too late, too impossible. His question wasn't born of rebellion but of resignation. Sometimes our hearts grow so accustomed to unanswered prayers that we stop believing the answer could actually come.

Yet here's the stunning truth: Zechariah's doubt didn't cancel God's plan. His unbelief didn't stop Elizabeth's pregnancy or John's birth. God's promises aren't dependent on our ability to wrap our minds around them. They rest on His character, not our confidence. The nine months of silence weren't punishment—they were preparation. Without words, Zechariah could only listen. Perhaps for the first time in his priestly life, he stopped speaking about God and started truly hearing from Him. When his voice finally returned, it erupted in prophecy and praise.

What impossible promise are you struggling to believe today? What prayer have you prayed so long that you've stopped expecting an answer? God specializes in bringing life where there's only barrenness. Your doubt may silence your voice for a season, but it cannot silence heaven's plan. God keeps every promise He makes. And as Zechariah's silent months passed, another promise—an even greater one—was drawing near. The world was about to receive its Savior.

Why not listen to this beautiful Christmas Hymn: "O come, O come, Emmanuel, and ransom captive Israel, that mourns in lonely exile here until the Son of God appear." – *O Come, O Come, Emmanuel*

Prayer:

Lord, forgive me when I doubt Your promises because my circumstances seem impossible. You spoke worlds into existence and bring life from barrenness. Strengthen my faith to believe Your Word even when I cannot see the way. When my prayers seem to go unanswered for years, help me trust that You are still working. May my life proclaim Your faithfulness, just as Zechariah's silence eventually gave way to praise. Amen

December 2 – Angel to Mary

by Pastor Greg Morris

"Then the angel told her, 'Do not be afraid, Mary, for you have found favor with God. Now listen: You will conceive and give birth to a son, and you will name him Jesus. He will be great and will be called the Son of the Most High, and the Lord God will give him the throne of his father David. He will reign over the house of Jacob forever, and his kingdom will have no end.' 'See, I am the Lord's servant,' said Mary. 'May it happen to me as you have said.'"
 – Luke 1:30–33, 38 (CSB)

"Mary's submission was not passive resignation but active cooperation with the will of God."
 – J.I. Packer

Reflection:

Mary was doing something ordinary—drawing water, grinding grain, mending clothes—when the impossible walked into her life. "Greetings, favored one! The Lord is with you."

She spun around, heart hammering. Gabriel stood before her, radiating power. "Do not be afraid, Mary. You have found favor with God. You will conceive and give birth to a son, and you are to call him Jesus. He will be great and will be called the Son of the Most High."

Mary's mind raced. She wasn't married. This would destroy her reputation, possibly her life. Joseph would have every right to divorce her. Yet her question wasn't *if* but *how*: "How will this be, since I am a virgin?"

When Gabriel explained that the Holy Spirit would overshadow her, Mary faced the defining choice of her young life. "I am the Lord's servant. May your word to me be fulfilled." Mary's "yes" is one of the most powerful statements in all of Scripture. She didn't say, "Let me think about it." She didn't ask for time to discuss it with her parents or Joseph. She didn't negotiate for better circumstances. She simply surrendered.

But let's not romanticize her decision. Mary understood the cost. In her culture, pregnancy outside marriage could mean death by stoning—at minimum, it meant scandal, shame, and social exile. She was choosing to become the subject of whispers, the target of judgment, the girl who "got herself in trouble." She was risking her engagement, her reputation, her entire future. Yet she said yes anyway.

Why? Because she believed God's character more than she feared her circumstances. She trusted that the One who called her "favored" would not abandon her to the consequences of obedience. She understood something profound: God wasn't asking for her ability—He was asking for her availability.

Mary didn't know about the refugee journey to Egypt ahead. She didn't know about the sword that would pierce her soul as she watched her son die. She didn't have all the information, and God didn't give her a detailed plan. He simply gave her an invitation, and she accepted.

What is God asking of you that requires faith before understanding? Where is He inviting your availability over your ability? The Christian life isn't about having all the answers—it's about trusting the One who does.

Sing or Play this beloved Christmas Hymn: "What child is this, who, laid to rest, on Mary's lap is sleeping? Whom angels greet with anthems sweet,

while shepherds watch are keeping?"
   – William Chatterton Dix, *What Child Is This?*

Prayer:

Heavenly Father, give me Mary's heart of surrender. When You call me to something beyond my understanding, help me trust Your character more than my circumstances. I confess that I often want all the details before I obey, all the answers before I move. Teach me that faith means saying yes to You even when the path ahead is unclear. Make me available for Your purposes. May my life echo Mary's words: "I am the Lord's servant." Amen.

December 3 – Angel to Joseph

by Pastor Greg Morris

"But after he had considered these things, an angel of the Lord appeared to him in a dream, saying, 'Joseph, son of David, don't be afraid to take Mary as your wife, because what has been conceived in her is from the Holy Spirit. She will give birth to a son, and you are to name him Jesus, because he will save his people from their sins.' When Joseph woke up, he did as the Lord's angel had commanded him. He married her."
– Matthew 1:20–21, 24 (CSB)

"Joseph's obedience was immediate, costly, and counter-cultural. He chose God's reputation over his own." – Max Lucado

Reflection:

Joseph's world was crumbling. The woman he loved was pregnant, and he knew the child wasn't his. The righteous thing, the legally protected thing, was to divorce her quietly. Tomorrow he would set the wheels in motion.

But that night, an angel appeared in his dreams: "Joseph, son of David, do not be afraid to take Mary home as your wife. What is conceived in her is from the Holy Spirit. She will give birth to a son, and you are to give him the name Jesus, because he will save his people from their sins."

When morning came, Joseph didn't deliberate. Scripture says simply: "He did what the angel of the Lord had commanded him." He took Mary as his wife.

We often overlook Joseph in the Christmas story, but his quiet obedience is staggering. Consider what he gave up with that single act of faith. He gave up his reputation as a righteous man. Everyone would assume he'd slept with Mary before marriage—or worse, that he was raising another man's child. His credibility in the community would be destroyed.

He gave up his own plans for marriage. Instead of the joyful wedding he'd anticipated, he'd face whispers and judgment. Instead of the honeymoon period every couple dreams of, he'd navigate pregnancy and childbirth surrounded by scandal. He gave up his right to be offended. Mary's pregnancy would have given him every legal and moral justification to walk away. Instead, he stepped forward.

And he did it all immediately. The text emphasizes his quick obedience: "When Joseph woke up, he did what the angel of the Lord had commanded him." No committee meetings. No cost-benefit analysis. No waiting to see if the situation would resolve itself. He simply obeyed. This is what faith looks like in work boots and a carpenter's apron. Not flashy or eloquent, not dramatic or attention-seeking. Just steady, costly, immediate obedience to God's voice.

Joseph teaches us that true obedience often requires sacrifice. Following God sometimes means doing what looks foolish to the world. It might cost you your reputation, your comfort, your carefully laid plans. But Joseph also teaches us that God honors those who honor Him. This quiet carpenter became the earthly father of the Son of God, forever remembered as the man who chose obedience over convenience. When God's instructions conflict with your plans or reputation, will you obey anyway?

Sing or play this beloved Christmas Hymn: "How silently, how silently, the wondrous gift is giv'n! So God imparts to human hearts the blessings of

His heav'n."

   – Phillips Brooks, *O Little Town of Bethlehem*

Prayer:

   Lord, give me Joseph's courage to obey You even when it costs me personally. Help me value Your approval above others' opinions. When Your call conflicts with my plans, my reputation, or my comfort, give me strength to choose Your way without hesitation. Teach me that quick obedience demonstrates trust in Your wisdom. Make me willing to look foolish for Your sake. Thank You for Joseph's example of quiet, steady faithfulness. Amen.

December 4 – Angels to Shepherds

by Pastor Greg Morris

"But the angel said to them, 'Don't be afraid, for look, I proclaim to you good news of great joy that will be for all the people. Today in the city of David a Savior was born for you, who is the Messiah, the Lord. This will be the sign for you: You will find a baby wrapped tightly in cloth and lying in a manger.' Suddenly there was a multitude of the heavenly host with the angel, praising God and saying: 'Glory to God in the highest heaven, and peace on earth to people he favors!'" – Luke 2:10– 14 (CSB)

"The God who roared the universe into existence came to earth in a stable so quiet you could hear the animals breathe." – Louie Giglio

Reflection:

The night was cold, the work tedious, the status low. Shepherds were the forgotten ones—too ceremonially unclean to worship in the temple, ranked barely above beggars in social hierarchy. They smelled like sheep, worked brutal hours, and were considered expendable.

Which made them perfect for what was about to happen.

The sheep were settled when the sky *ripped open*. Light exploded across the hills. The shepherds hit the ground; certain they were about to die. "Do not be afraid! I bring you good news that will cause great joy for all the people. Today in the town of David a Savior has been born to you; he is the Messiah, the Lord."

Before they could process it, the single angel multiplied into thousands. The heavenly host filled the sky: "Glory to God in the highest heaven, and on earth peace to those on whom his favor rests!" Then—silence. Darkness. The ordinary night returned, but nothing would ever be ordinary again. "Let's go to Bethlehem," one gasped. And they ran.

Stop and consider the scandal of this moment. The birth announcement of the King of Kings, the arrival of the long-awaited Messiah, the most important event in human history—and God's first phone call went to shepherds. Not to Herod in his palace. Not to the high priest in Jerusalem. Not to the scholars who'd spent their lives studying prophecies about this very moment. God bypassed the powerful, the educated, the religious elite, and chose the nobodies.

This reveals something fundamental about God's kingdom: it's upside-down from the world's system. The first are last. The last are first. The overlooked are chosen. The forgotten are sought. The outcasts are welcomed.

But there's more here. The shepherds didn't clean themselves up before running to Bethlehem. They didn't go home to change clothes or rehearse what they'd say. They went *as they were*—dirty, smelly, unqualified, inappropriate. And when they arrived at that stable, they found a King who didn't care about their résumé or their reputation. He welcomed their worship.

If you've ever felt like you're on the outside looking in, remember this moment. If you've ever thought you're too broken, too ordinary, too far from God to matter—the shepherds demolish that lie. You don't need status to receive the gospel. You don't need education to understand grace. You don't need to clean up before coming to Jesus.

The greatest news in human history came first to those who had nothing to offer but themselves. That's still how it works. God doesn't need your perfection—He wants your presence. Come as you are.

Sing or Play this beloved Christmas Hymn: "Hark! the herald angels sing, 'Glory to the newborn King! Peace on earth, and mercy mild, God and sinners reconciled!'"

– Charles Wesley, *Hark! The Herald Angels Sing*

Prayer:

Father, thank You that Your good news is for ordinary people like me. I don't have to earn the right to come to You or be important in the world's eyes to matter to You. Forgive me when I think I need to get my life together before approaching You. Help me run to Jesus just as I am, like the shepherds who left their fields to worship the newborn King. May I never lose the wonder of this good news that brings great joy. Amen.

December 5 – Prophecies Fulfilled

by Pastor Greg Morris

"For a child will be born for us,
a son will be given to us,
and the government will be on his shoulders.
He will be named
Wonderful Counselor, Mighty God,
Eternal Father, Prince of Peace." - Isaiah 9:6

"Every prophecy fulfilled in Christ is God's signature on the document of redemption, proving that He keeps His promises across centuries." – A.W. Tozer

Reflection:

For seven hundred years, Isaiah's words had echoed: "The virgin will conceive and give birth to a son, and they will call him Immanuel"—God with us. For seven hundred years, Micah had pointed to Bethlehem: "Though you are small among the clans of Judah, out of you will come... one who will be ruler over Israel." And Isaiah's magnificent declaration: "For to us a child is born... And he will be called Wonderful Counselor, Mighty God, Everlasting Father, Prince of Peace."

Generation after generation recited these prophecies. Grandparents told grandchildren. Rabbis taught students. The faithful clung to these promises through exile and oppression. Some lost hope. Many forgot.

13

Then, in a single night, centuries of prophecy collapsed into present reality. A virgin conceived—in Bethlehem. A child born who was somehow divine. Every detail, every impossible prediction, every ancient promise came together perfectly.

This wasn't coincidence. This was orchestration.

Imagine being part of the generation that waited seven hundred years for a promise. Your great-great-great-grandparents heard the prophecy. They believed it, taught it to their children, and died without seeing it fulfilled. Their children did the same. And their children. And theirs. Century after century, the promise hung in the air, unfulfilled but not forgotten.

How long do you stay faithful to a promise that spans seven centuries? How do you keep believing when everyone who first heard the prophecy is long dead? When empires rise and fall, and still the promise hasn't come?

Yet God was working the entire time. Every year that passed wasn't delay—it was preparation. The stage was being set. The Roman roads that would carry the gospel were being built. The Greek language that would communicate truth across cultures was spreading. The Jewish diaspora that would seed the early church was scattering. Even the census that brought Mary and Joseph to Bethlehem was part of the grand design.

God's timing is never late. It's often later than we want, but it's always exactly on schedule. What feels like divine delay is actually divine design.

What promise are you waiting for God to fulfill? Perhaps you've prayed for years with no answer. Perhaps you're starting to wonder if God even heard you. The prophecies of Christ's birth shout this truth across the centuries: God always keeps His promises, even when the fulfillment takes longer than a lifetime.

Your job isn't to figure out the timeline. It's not to understand the how or the when. Your job is simply to keep believing. To hold onto hope even in the silence. To pass the promise to the next generation if necessary, trusting that God's Word never returns void.

The wait was seven hundred years. But when the moment came, every detail was perfect. Worth the wait doesn't begin to describe it.

Sing or Play this beautiful Christmas Hymn: "Come, Thou long expected Jesus, born to set Thy people free; from our fears and sins release us, let us find our rest in Thee."

– Charles Wesley, *Come, Thou Long Expected Jesus*

Prayer:

Faithful God, You are the Promise Keeper who spans generations to fulfill Your Word. Thank You that Jesus is the proof of Your faithfulness—every prophecy fulfilled, every promise kept. When I grow weary in waiting, when the silence stretches long and I wonder if You've forgotten, remind me of Your perfect timing. Strengthen my faith to trust that what You have promised, You will bring to pass— even if it takes longer than my lifetime. Help me to wait with hope, knowing that You are always at work, always orchestrating, always faithful. Amen.

December 6 - Mary's "Yes" To God

by Pastor Aaron Routon

38 And Mary said, "Behold, I am the servant of the Lord; let it be to me according to your word." And the angel departed from her. - Luke 1:38 ESV

"When obedience to God contradicts what I think will give me pleasure, let me ask myself if I love Him"
  - Elisabeth Elliot

Reflection:
   Saying Yes to God is a theme throughout the scriptures. Noah, Abraham, Moses, David, Isaiah, Mary, AND Jesus(Philippians 2:2-11) said "YES" to the Lord. Each of these Biblical icons encountered a moment, an opportunity, to say "Yes" to the call of the Lord or turn Him down. Not one of them said "Yes" because there was a chance at fame and fortune. Their obedience came from an encounter with and a faith in God.

Mary's "Yes" shows the understanding she had of her position. She did not see herself as "The chosen one", but as a servant being called upon to carry a great responsibility. There was no personal gain to be had for a teenage girl pregnant out of wedlock. In the world her "Yes" meant she may face social ridicule, shame, and exile. But in the Kingdom of God the result of her "yes" far outweighed any difficulty she may endure because of it.

Her response, "Let it be according to Your Word" shows her trust in God's plan. She did not fully understand how God's plan would unfold. She had no foreknowledge of the manger birth, Herod's murder of innocent children, fleeing to Egypt, and the eventual death of her firstborn son. However, there was a confidence in God that He would lead her through every moment. I am sure that Noah had no idea just how much rain would fall, and Moses did not see the plagues, the sea, or the wilderness; but they knew that God's Word was the best word to have unfold in their lives.

What act of obedience is God asking from you today? Is it to obey His commands? (John 14:15). Is He asking you to be a more committed disciple or to step into an area of ministry? Or is it something as simple as loving your neighbor? Do you trust that His call also comes with His protection?

Take up the challenge and give God a sincere "YES" to His call today.

Prayer:

Lord I thank you for asking me to be a part of your work in this life. Today, I am your humble servant and I say "YES" to You! Here I am, send me. I trust your plan, even when I do not understand and cannot see the end goal. I know that You alone are sovereign and will make my paths straight. Help me to hear your instructions clearly and to obey you completely. I choose to serve You no matter what others may think or say about me. Let Your will be done in my life. Amen.

December 7 - Obedience in Uncertainty

by Pastor Aaron Routon

19 And her husband Joseph, since he was a righteous man and did not want to disgrace her, planned to send her away secretly. 20 But when he had thought this over, behold, an angel of the Lord appeared to him in a dream, saying, "Joseph, son of David, do not be afraid to take Mary as your wife; for the Child who has been conceived in her is of the Holy Spirit. - Matthew 1:19-20

"Because He lives, I can face tomorrow,
  Because He lives, all fear is gone;
  Because I know He holds the future,
  And life is worth the living just because He lives" - Gloria Gaither/William J. Gaither © 1971 Hanna Street Music

Reflection:

Imagine yourself for a moment in Joseph's predicament. He had the career and a blossoming relationship with marriage on the horizon when all of his plans suddenly became pointless. The culture of the time period gave Joseph clear instruction on the procedures for his fiancé's surprise pregnancy, but God would have different instructions for Joseph.

Uncertainty is a nice way of describing other emotions such as worry, anxiety, and fear. These are things we deal with when we do not know what is happening, why it is happening, or what lies ahead. We cannot know for sure what flurry of feelings washed over Joseph with Mary's revelation of pregnancy. It would be understandable if uncertainty was among them, but Joseph's handling of the whole situation shows us what to do in these moments.

He first believed the Word of the Lord. When Joseph awoke from his angelic dream he could have moved forward in disbelief. Yet in this moment he chose to believe the Word of the Lord. In the throws of life's uncertainties, belief or faith in God and His word is vital to the believer not being overcome with worry and fear.

Secondly, Joseph obeyed the Word of the Lord. Seemingly without delay, Joseph did as he was commanded and continued not in uncertainty but with steadfast action. (Matt.1:24). When confronted with variables concerning our present or future, obedience will be the constant for the believer.

Lastly, the modern day God follower has something that Joseph did not…We have the risen Lord! Despite the uncertainties of life one thing remains true, our King is on the Throne. Jesus is seated at the Right hand of the Father making intercession for us. (Rom. 8:24, Heb. 7:25) Today we can be CERTAIN that our sovereign Lord has everything under control!

Prayer:
Lord, thank You for the reminder that even in seasons of uncertainty, You are steady, faithful, and fully in control. Just as You spoke courage and clarity to Joseph, speak to our hearts today. Help us to believe Your Word when circumstances don't make sense. Give us the strength to obey quickly, even when the path ahead feels unclear. Teach us to rest in the truth that because Jesus lives, we can face tomorrow without fear. May we walk forward today with assurance that our King is on the throne and nothing in our lives is beyond Your care. In Jesus' name, Amen.

December 8 - Mary's Song of Praise

by Pastor Aaron Routon

46 And Mary said,"My soul magnifies the Lord, 47
and my spirit rejoices in God my Savior,
Luke 1:46-47

"Our heavenly Father loves us with an extravagant abandon. Passionate, undigni-
fied worship is our only reasonable response."
– Matt Redman

Reflection:

It is in Mary's song of praise that we see her response to all that has been unfolding in her life. Growing within her womb is the One whom the prophets wrote about. This baby boy is the Messiah, and Mary knows it. She understands the greatness that is the fulfillment of thousands of years of prophecy. It is in this moment in Luke 1:46-55 that Mary's spirit is so overwhelmed with humility and joy that praise erupts from within her.

Her song praises the God who uses the Humble things to upset the prideful arrogant order of the world. Paul would write something similar to this in 1st Corinthians 1:27; "but God has chosen the foolish things of the world to shame the wise, and God has chosen the weak things of the world to shame the things which are strong,". It is by using the unexpected things that God receives great glory.

He often chooses those who might seem small, insignificant, undereducated, and too damaged. It is through the redemption of these that God shows His greatness. Take a moment and recall the things that God has rescued you from. When you accepted Christ as your savior a new birth occurred within you. The prophet Ezekiel described it as replacing a heart of stone with a heart of flesh. (Ezk. 36:26). The Apostle Paul talks about all things being made new. (2nd Cor. 5:17)

God has done something miraculous within the life of every believer. He has done the impossible! He has created new life within us and we have been born again! Our sins are washed away! Knowing this, how can we remain silent? If we truly understand the work that God has done then our hearts should erupt with praise. The breath in our lungs ought to shout with praise for who He is and what He has done! Let Everything that has breath praise the Lord!

Prayer:

Thank You Jesus for saving me! Thank you for bringing me out of darkness into Your marvelous light. Thank you for your great mercy and forgiveness of sin. I rejoice in God my Savior. You are mighty. You have done great things. Holy is your name. Let me never grow callused to giving you the praise you deserve and fill me with the desire to magnify Your name.

December 9 - Obey Without Delay

by Pastor Aaron Routon

13 Now when they had gone, behold, an angel of the Lord *appeared to Joseph in a dream and said, "Get up! Take the Child and His mother and flee to Egypt, and stay there until I tell you; for Herod is going to search for the Child to kill Him." -Matthew 2:13 NASB

"If you look up into His face and say, "Yes, Lord, whatever it costs," at that moment He'll flood your Life with His presence and power." - Alan Redpath

Reflection:

Joseph was charged with being the protector of his family. Like any parent, despite the fact that this child carried some serious significance, the goal was to defend Him at all cost. How watchful we are of the precious things God has entrusted into our care. Yet while we sleep our father in Heaven stands as defender over us.

God's way of protecting this young family was to entrust Jesus' earthly father with guidance that would remove them from the path of Herod's wrath. I am not one for speculation, but what might have happened if Joseph had chosen to delay in his following of God's direction? Thankfully the outcome is without debate as Joseph acted immediately in taking his wife and child to Egypt.

Through Joseph's story we can ascertain that he was a man of good character and devout faith in The Most High God. His deep faith led to his acts of obedience. If you truly believe then you will obey. (John 14:15) Your obedience ties you to the life of Jesus, and reveals your dedication and devotion. Our obedience to what the Word has said is a declaration of our faith. (James 2:14-24)

Can God entrust you with His words of guidance that may impact someone's life? Be aware that God is still speaking. If you are devoted to Him and full of His Spirit then He may call on you to act on His behalf. Will you listen and obey If God were to speak to you to pray a specific prayer for your family or someone you know? Do not delay, your prayer, your word of encouragement, or just checking in on someone at the direction of the Spirit may have life altering implications. Do not delay...OBEY.

Prayer:

Lord I want to be obedient to your word today. Fill me with Your Spirit and help me to discern your voice. Let my character be trustworthy. Let my obedience be swift. Use me as an asset for your providential work in the lives of others. Your plan is perfect and I desire to walk in Your way. Wake me up, interrupt my day, and speak to my heart so that I may do the work that you need me to do. Amen.

December 10 - Lessons In Trust and Surrender

by Pastor Aaron Routon

"Trust in the Lord with all your heart, and do not lean on your own understanding. In all your ways acknowledge him, and he will make straight your paths"
  Proverbs 3:5-6 (ESV)

"If my life is surrendered to God, all is well. Let me not grab it back, as though it were in peril in His hand but would be safer in mine!"
  Elisabeth Elliot

Reflection:

There are many things within the pages of the scriptures that leave us asking for more. Of course we trust in God but that does not quench our human instinct to ask "why?".

There is an inherent need to know everything, all the details, to have complete understanding. As we read the Advent story surrounding Mary and Joseph we see only one response that involved a question. (Luke 1:34) Every encounter implies that these two had complete trust in and surrender to the direction of the Lord.

Mary and Joseph were not chosen because they looked the part or had the most lucrative family connections. No, they were chosen because of the content of their heart. God knew they would act with humility. He knew they viewed themselves as obedient servants. He knew they would trust Him wholeheartedly therefore He could trust them with an immense responsibility. I believe God knew that they would not become caught up with the ego of being the parents of the Messiah, and remain in total surrender to His plan.

What about us? Do we find ourselves asking "Why"? Are we overwhelmed with the need to see the entire blueprint of the future? What if today we were to trust in the Lord with our WHOLE heart?

You are chosen for something wonderful in this life but God's plan will always require trust and surrender. Trust in His plans and the surrendering of ours of His. You do not have to LOOK like someone God can use, you just need a heart that is unwaveringly devoted to follow Him.

Prayer:

Jesus, I trust in You with all my heart. I cannot possibly understand everything that happens or will happen, but I WILL trust You through every moment. I trust the plan you have laid out for my life and I surrender to your desired will. Thank you for giving my life purpose and meaning. You are the one who guides my life. Have Your way in me. Amen.

December 11 - Shepherds Chosen

by Pastor T.J. Smith

"In the same region, shepherds were staying out in the fields and keeping watch at night over their flock. Then an angel of the Lord stood before them, and the glory of the Lord shone around them, and they were terrified." - Luke 2:8–9 (CSB)

"The angels are singing over the plains
The shepherds are quaking, echoing refrains (Echoing refrains)
And all of our slogans designed to take away the pain
Meant nothing to the Son of God that night in Bethlehem" - Five Iron Frenzy

Reflection:

It was an unremarkable night in an overlooked town. It felt like every other night. Yet in that quiet moment, the King of Kings entered human history. And when heaven chose its first audience, it wasn't the upper class. It was shepherds. Ordinary men doing an ordinary job on an ordinary night. That's the grace of God on full display.

We like to think we can get through the darkness with a few good quotes or positive affirmations. We say things like, "You've got this," or "Everything happens for a reason." But the truth is, our slogans can't save us. They can't lift the weight of sin, fix the human heart, or conquer death. The slogans meant nothing to Jesus that night in Bethlehem because He didn't come to give us better words or a new form of enlightenment—He came to give us Himself.

He wasn't born to inspire temporary hope; He was born with eternal purpose. The world didn't need another good teacher; it needed a Savior. In that moment, God's message was unmistakable: real hope would never come from human effort but from divine intervention. And it started with light breaking into the darkness, announced to shepherds who never expected to be part of the story.

If you've ever felt worn out, unseen, or like you're just trying to make it through another day, remember that's where God showed up first. He still steps into our everyday lives, right in the middle of our routines, our exhaustion, and our uncertainty, to remind us He hasn't forgotten us. When our own words fall short, His Word comes alive. And that changes everything.

Prayer:

Jesus, thank You for coming when the world was lost in darkness. You didn't send another message of hope; You became our hope. Help me not to settle for empty words or quick fixes when You've already given me what I truly need. You have given us Your salvation and light. Remind me that You choose ordinary people, and that Your glory still breaks into the darkest nights. Amen.

December 12 - Shepherds Respond

by Pastor T.J. Smith

"When the angels had left them and returned to heaven, the shepherds said to one another, 'Let's go straight to Bethlehem and see what has happened, which the Lord has made known to us.' They hurried off and found both Mary and Joseph, and the baby who was lying in the manger." - Luke 2:15–16 (CSB)

"He went to the shepherds—men who didn't have a reputation to protect, an axe to grind, or a ladder to climb ... men who didn't know enough to tell God that angels don't sing to sheep and that Messiahs are not found wrapped in rags and sleeping in a feed trough."
— Max Lucado, God Came Near

Reflection:

The shepherds didn't sit around talking about what they had just seen. They didn't form a committee or make a list of questions to ask God. They simply said, *"Let's go."* It's easy to read that and think, *Of course they went!* Angels had just appeared to them, lighting up the sky. But these men still had sheep to watch, responsibilities to keep, and lives that didn't usually include anything this supernatural. Yet they knew this wasn't just another night. God had broken into their world, and nothing would ever be the same.

They weren't scholars or priests. They didn't have influence, titles, or religious training. They weren't the kind of people anyone expected to see in the middle of a divine miracle. But maybe that's exactly why God chose them. They didn't have an image to protect. They just had open hearts.

When God showed up, they didn't argue. They didn't ask for more proof or pretend to understand every detail. They simply believed and obeyed. And because they did, they got to witness something some would never get to see. They saw the Savior of the world lying in a manger.

Faith doesn't always mean understanding everything; it means trusting that what God says is true even when you can't see the whole picture. It's choosing to move forward when the details are unclear because you trust the One who's calling you to move. Sometimes we like to know where things are going before we take the first step. We want God to hand us the plan before we trust the process. But that's not how faith always works. Faith means taking the next step even when you don't see the whole road yet. That's what the shepherds did. They didn't know what they'd find in Bethlehem, but they went anyway. They trusted that if God had spoken, it was worth following.

You might not feel ready or qualified. Maybe you look at your life and think, *Why would God choose me?* But that's the point. God doesn't look for people with the best accomplishments. He looks for people who are willing to listen. The shepherds were ordinary, but they were listened, and that was enough.

They could have stayed in the fields. They could have talked themselves out of it or convinced each other it wasn't real. But they didn't. They acted on what they heard. And once they encountered Jesus, they couldn't keep it to themselves. That's what happens when you really meet Him, you don't walk the same.

God still speaks today. You might hear Him through Scripture, through a moment that stirs your heart, or through that quiet nudge you can't shake.

When He does, don't brush it off or talk yourself out of it. Every time you respond to His voice, you step further into the purpose He created you for. What could be better than walking in that?

Prayer:

Lord, help me to have the kind of faith that moves. When You speak, I don't want to stay where I am. Teach me to respond with trust even when I don't have all the answers. Thank You for showing Yourself to people like the shepherds—and like me. Let my response to You bring You glory today. Amen.

December 13 – Wise Men's Journey

by Pastor T.J. Smith

"After Jesus was born in Bethlehem of Judea in the days of King Herod, wise men from the east arrived in Jerusalem, saying, 'Where is he who has been born king of the Jews? For we saw his star at its rising and have come to worship him.'" - *Matthew 2:1–2 (CSB)*

"You wonder if this star won't stop in the dark. You wonder if you did the whole walk on a farce. And I could feel that too. Tryna see it as He's leading me through. Keep your eyes on the Star and you'll be dreamin' it too. And keep the frankincense handy, you'll be needin' it soon. He's got redeemin' to do." — Paul Russell

Reflection:

The wise men's story is one of faith, endurance, and pursuit. They didn't have all the answers. They saw a star rise in the sky and believed it meant something. They studied the signs, packed their gifts, and began a long, uncertain journey toward someone they had never met. There's no record that they knew exactly where they were going or how long it would take. They just followed the light.

Sometimes we might wonder if the walk is worth it. How many times have we felt that way? You start following God, trusting His direction, and then the road seems quiet. You wonder if you misheard Him. You wonder if the light you thought you saw was just a flicker of your own imagination.

But the wise men kept going. Even when the journey didn't make sense, even when the star seemed distant, they kept their eyes fixed on what God had revealed. That's what faith is. It's movement based on trust, not proof.

Sometimes we want the full plan before we start. We want God to show us the destination, the timing, and the results. But faith doesn't work like that. God sometimes gives us just enough light to take the next step. The wise men didn't know how close they were when they reached Jerusalem. They asked questions, followed the clues, and eventually found themselves in front of a small child in a simple home. Not a palace. Not the setting they expected. But they knew the presence of the King when they saw Him.

When they finally arrived, they bowed in worship. Not because they felt obligated, but because they understood something holy had been unfolding all along. Every mile, every sleepless night, every moment of uncertainty had been preparing them for this encounter. The journey hadn't been wasted; it was the means by which they came to know the Savior.

It's the same for us. God doesn't waste the waiting or the wandering moments of our lives. The moments that feel slow or confusing are often the very places He's shaping our faith. We think the goal is just to arrive, but with God, the journey itself is part of the redemption. Every delay, every prayer we think is unanswered, and every quiet night is drawing us deeper into trust.

The same God who guided the wise men through the dark still leads His people today. And when the light finally stops, when you see where He's been leading, you'll realize He was never far off. You'll find Jesus there, redeeming what you couldn't fix, fulfilling what you could only hope for, and proving once again that He's the destination every heart is searching for.

Prayer:

Lord, help me keep my eyes on You even when the journey feels long. When the light seems far away, remind me that You're still leading. Strengthen my faith when I start to doubt, and help me trust that every step of obedience is drawing me closer to You. Thank You for being the Redeemer who never loses sight of those who follow Your light. Amen.

December 14 – Wise Men Obey God, Not Herod

by Pastor T.J. Smith

"And being warned in a dream not to go back to Herod, they returned to their own country by another route." - Matthew 2:12 (CSB)

"There are two ways to deal with Jesus: the way of Herod, and the way of the wise men. The way of Herod is to get rid of Jesus. It was pure hypocrisy when Herod said he wanted to go worship the child. He did not intend to worship him. He intended to get rid of him. And in a matter of days, he would kill every baby boy in Bethlehem under two years old to get rid of Jesus. He failed. Herod's way always fails."
— *John Piper*

Reflection:

The wise men didn't just worship, they obeyed. After their encounter with the child, God warned them in a dream not to return to Herod, and they listened. They changed their route. They went home a different way, both physically and spiritually.

Worship changes what direction we're going. When you really meet Jesus, you can't go back to life as it was before. You begin to see things differently. You make decisions differently. You start following His voice instead of the world's.

Herod represents a different kind of response. He heard about Jesus too. He even pretended to care. He told the wise men, *"Go and search carefully for the child, and when you find him, report back to me so that I too can go and worship him."* But really it was about fear and control. Herod wasn't interested in bowing to Jesus. He was threatened by the idea of another king.

There are still two ways to respond to Jesus today. You can respond like Herod, protecting your own throne, or like the wise men, surrendering to His. One response tries to control God; the other submits to Him. One leads to destruction; the other leads to joy.

The wise men could have gone back to Herod. It would have been the easier choice, the safer choice, the one that made sense politically. But they didn't. They trusted what God said, even when it disrupted their plans. That's obedience. It's not always convenient, but it's always right.

Sometimes God will ask you to take a different route too. It might not make sense to anyone else, but when you've truly encountered Jesus, you start caring more about His approval than anyone else's. The road of obedience often costs you something, but it always leads you closer to Him.

Herod's way always fails in the end. You can resist Jesus, ignore Him, or try to keep Him at a safe distance, but He is the King. His kingdom doesn't fade, and His authority doesn't bend to ours. The wise men understood that, and it changed everything about their journey.

So the question is: what do we do with Jesus when He disrupts our plans? Do we protect our comfort, or do we trust Him? The wise men show us the better way. Obedience is never wasted, even when it's costly. God's warned the wise men to lead them safely home. His direction always leads to life.

Prayer:

Lord, help me to respond to You like the wise men did. When You speak, I don't want to argue or hesitate. I want to listen and obey. Keep my heart from being like Herod's and protecting my own way instead of surrendering to Yours. Lead me down the path that honors You, even when it means taking a different route. Amen.

December 15 - Worship Through Giving

by Pastor T.J. Smith

"Entering the house, they saw the child with Mary his mother, and falling to their knees, they worshiped him. Then they opened their treasures and presented him with gifts: gold, frankincense, and myrrh." - Matthew 2:11 (CSB)

"If you have gold, then give it; if you have frankincense, then give it; if you have myrrh, then give it to Jesus; if you don't have any of these things, give Him your love—all of your love—and that will be gold and spices all in one. Give Him your tongue, speak of Him; give Him your hands, work for Him; give Him your whole self. I know you will, for He loved you and gave Himself for you." — Charles Spurgeon

Reflection:

The wise men didn't give to earn anything from God. They gave because they knew who stood before them. Their gifts were a way of saying, "You are worthy." That's what real giving is. It's not about impressing God or doing the right thing. It's about recognizing that everything you have already belongs to Him.

When you've truly seen Jesus for who He is, giving becomes natural. It's not forced or complicated. You start wanting to use what you have to honor Him. When your heart changes, so does the way you live. You start to see your time, your money, your words, and your effort as opportunities to honor God.

The wise men came to give, but the child they knelt before would one day give far more. The same Jesus who received their gifts would later give Himself for the world. He would give His life to rescue us from sin and bring us back to God. He offered the ultimate gift, Himself.

That's what shapes how we give today. We don't give to get something in return. We give because God gave first. Every act of generosity, every moment of serving, and every time you give from your heart is a reminder that you belong to a Savior who gave everything for you.

Giving like that isn't about losing anything. It's about becoming more like Him. It reminds us that life isn't about holding on but about trusting the One who already gave us more than we could ever deserve. When we live that way, we start to see that nothing we give to Jesus is ever wasted.

Prayer:

Jesus, You are the greatest giver. Every good thing I have comes from You. Teach me to give like You give. You give freely, joyfully, and from the heart. Help me to see that when I offer You my love, my time, and my life, I'm only giving back what You first gave me. Thank You for giving Yourself so I could have life. Amen.

December 16 - Herod's Fear

by Pastor William Reid

"When King Herod heard this, he was disturbed, and all Jerusalem with him." — *Matthew 2:3 (NIV)*

Reflection:

The birth of Jesus was announced with joy to shepherds, awe to wise men, and fear to a king. King Herod ruled with cruelty and cunning. He was deeply protective of his power, and when the Magi arrived in Jerusalem asking, *"Where is the one who has been born king of the Jews?"* Herod was disturbed— and not just him, but *"all Jerusalem with him."*

Why would a baby cause a king to tremble?

Herod wasn't afraid of a child. He was afraid of a **kingdom**—a new reign that might challenge his own. Even though Jesus was born in humility, with no army or palace, Herod sensed something dangerous: **a threat to the throne of self.**

In many ways, Herod's fear is not so foreign. Jesus doesn't come to merely inspire or comfort; **He comes to rule.** His presence disrupts every lesser kingdom we build—kingdoms of pride, control, reputation, and comfort.

Herod's tragic response was to resist and try to destroy what God was doing.

He chose control over surrender, violence over worship, fear over faith. We face the same challenges and are called upon to make Godly choices.

Reflection Questions:

- What part of my life feels "disturbed" by Jesus' call to surrender?
- Am I clinging to control where God is calling me to trust?
- Is there a "throne" in my heart that needs to be given back to its rightful King?
- How does Jesus' eternal kingship give you peace in a violent and chaotic world?

Prayer:

Lord Jesus, You are the true King. Forgive me for the ways I've resisted Your reign in my life. I confess my fears and my desire to hold onto control.

Teach me to welcome You not with resistance like Herod, but with worship like the wise men. May Your kingdom come in my heart as it is in heaven. Amen.

December 17 - Massacre of Innocents

by Pastor William Reid

"Then Herod, when he saw that he had been deceived by the wise men, was exceedingly angry; and he sent forth and put to death all the male children who were in Bethlehem and in all its districts, from two years old and under..." (NKJV) - Matthew 2:13–14

Reflection:

Even in the beauty of Christ's birth, darkness tried to destroy the Light. Herod's cruelty shows how deeply sin corrupts the human heart. The same world that welcomed angels and shepherds also witnessed weeping mothers in Bethlehem. Evil does not rest even at the birth of the Savior. **John 1:5 –** *"The light shines in darkness, and the darkness has not overcome it."*

Though Herod sought to destroy, God sent an angel to Joseph in a dream, saying, "Arise, take the young Child and His mother, flee to Egypt" (v. 13). God was already working behind the scenes to protect His plan of salvation. God's purposes are never defeated by human evil.

Romans 8:28 – *"And we know that all things work together for good to those who love God."*

Christmas is a season of joy, but it's also a reminder that God entered a world of pain and injustice. The cries of the mothers of Bethlehem are heard by a

God who also weeps with His people. **Matthew quotes Jeremiah 31:15** – *"A voice was heard in Ramah, lamentation, weeping, and great mourning."* **Hebrews 4:15 says** – *"For we do not have a High Priest who cannot sympathize with our weaknesses."*

Herod's reign of terror ended in death, but Christ's kingdom endures forever. Earthly power is temporary; divine purpose is eternal. Jesus, the true King, conquers not by violence but through love and sacrifice. **Revelation 11:15** – *"The kingdoms of this world have become the kingdoms of our Lord and of His Christ."*

Even through tragedy, God's redemptive plan unfolds. The massacre of the innocents reminds us that suffering does not cancel God's promises—it magnifies our need for the Savior. The same Jesus who escaped death as a child would later face death on the cross to us all. **Romans 15:13** – *"May the God of hope fill you with all joy and peace in believing."*

The "Massacre of the Innocents" reminds us that Christmas is not just about joy and light; it's about God entering a dark and painful world to bring hope. The tears of Bethlehem are not forgotten; they are redeemed by the blood of the Lamb.

Reflection Questions:

- Why do you think evil often tries hardest to work when God is doing something powerful?
- How has God protected or redirected your life to fulfill His purpose?
- What does it mean to you that God understands and feels your pain?
- How does Jesus' eternal kingship give your peace in a violent and chaotic world?
- How can you bring hope to others who are hurting this Christmas season?

Prayer:

"Lord Jesus, You came onto a broken world full of pain and injustice. Help us to see Your light even in our darkest moments. May Your peace rule in our hearts, and may we share Your hope with a world in need. Amen."

December 18 - Darkness Tries To Silence Light

by Pastor William Reid

"In Him was life, and the life was the light of man. The light shines in the darkness, and the darkness has not overcome it." - John 1:4–5 (ESV)

Reflection:

The world Jesus entered was filled with corruption, opposition, and spiritual blindness. Yet, into that very darkness, God sent His Light—His Son! The manger in Bethlehem glowed with the hope of salvation. God's plan to redeem the world began quietly, but it carried eternal power. **Luke 2:11** – *"For unto you is born this day in the city of David a Savior who is Christ the Lord."*

From the beginning, evil forces tried to silence the Light. Herod's massacre of the innocents, Satan's temptations, and ultimately the crucifixion all revealed the world's attempt to extinguish Jesus. Darkness always resists truth. But every time darkness attacks, the Light shines brighter. **John 8:12** – *"I am the light of the world. Whoever follows Me will not walk in darkness but will have the light of life."*

No matter how fierce the opposition, **darkness cannot defeat light.** When Jesus was crucified, it seemed the Light was done, but the Resurrection proved otherwise. Every Christmas reminds us: The Light still shines. **1 John 2:8 –** *"The darkness is passing away, and the true light is already shining."*

Jesus calls His followers to reflect His light. Christmas is not only about celebrating the birth of Christ, it's about becoming His witnesses in a dark world. The light that shines in you is meant to shine through you. **Matthew 5:14–16 –** *"You are the light of the world... Let your light shine before others."*

Christmas points us to eternity—a future where darkness will be no more. The Light that began in Bethlehem will one day fill the entire world. In heaven, there will be no more night, no more tears, and no more darkness. **Revelation 22:5 –** *"They need no light of lamp or sun, for the Lord God will be their light."*

Every Christmas, the battle between darkness and light is remembered, but we celebrate knowing who wins. The Manger reminds us that no matter how deep the night, **the light of Christ cannot be silenced.**

Reflection Questions:

- How does the light of Christ shine in your life when things seem dark?
- What forms of "darkness" do you see trying to silence Christ's light in our world today?
- How can you stand firm when the darkness of doubt, fear, or sin tries to silence your faith?
- How can you let Christ's light shine through your words, actions, and attitude this Christmas?
- What hope does the promise of eternal light bring to you this Christmas season?

Prayer:

"Lord Jesus, You are the light that no darkness can overcome. When fear, sin, or sorrow try to silence our faith, remind us that Your light still shines. Help us to be bearers of Your light in a dark world this Christmas and always. Amen."

December 19 - Protection

by Pastor William Reid

"Now when they had departed, behold, an Angel of the Lord appeared to Joseph in a dream, saying, 'Arise, take the young child and his mother, flee to Egypt, and stay there until I bring you word; for Herod will seek the young child to destroy him.'" - Matthew 2:13

Reflection:

From the very beginning, God's plan of salvation faced threats. King Herod tried to destroy the newborn King, but God's plan would not be stopped. God sent an angel to warn Joseph and Mary to flee to Egypt. No human power can ever destroy what God has decreed. **Isaiah 14:27** – *"The LORD Almighty has purposed, and who can thwart Him?"*

Just as God watched over Mary, Joseph, and the infant Jesus, He watches over His people today. God's protection doesn't mean life will always be easy—it means He will always be present. Even in difficult circumstances, God shields, guides, and sustains His children. **Isaiah 41:10** – *"Fear not, for I am with you; be not dismayed for I am your God."*

God didn't just protect Joseph and Mary; He guided them every step of the way through dreams and divine direction. God's protection often comes through His guidance. When we listen to His voice, He leads us safely through danger and uncertainty. **Proverbs 3:5–6** – *"Trust in the Lord with all your heart... And He shall direct your paths."*

The journey to Egypt was not random—it fulfilled prophecy: *"Out of Egypt I called My Son"* (**Matthew 2:15; Hosea 11:1**). God's protection always works in harmony with His promises. Every step of Joseph's obedience fulfills Scripture and secured the future of salvation. **2 Thessalonians 3:3** says, *"The Lord is faithful, who will establish you and guard you from the evil one."*

God's protection is never random—it always has purpose. He protected Jesus so the Savior could fulfill His mission, to bring light and life to all. The same God who protected the Child in Bethlehem protects your life for a reason. His purpose for you is unfolding even now.

Reflection Questions

- When has God protected or redirected your life to fulfill His purpose?
- What does it mean to trust God's protection even when the path isn't easy?
- How can you recognize God's hand guiding you in small, everyday ways?
- What does this story teach you about God's power to fulfill His promises?
- How can you thank God today for the ways He's protected and guided you?

Prayer:

"Lord, thank You for watching over my life with divine care. Help me to trust Your protection and guidance, even when I don't understand the path ahead. Like Joseph, help me to obey quickly and trust fully. Thank You that no plan of Yours can be stopped. Amen."

December 20 - Jesus, Light in the Darkness

by Pastor William Reid

"In Him was life, and the life was the light of men. The light shines in the darkness, and the darkness has not overcome it." - John 1:4–5 (ESV)

Before Jesus came, the world was filled with spiritual darkness, sin, oppression, and hopelessness. Humanity stumbled, searching for meaning and direction. But God did not leave us in the dark—He sent His Son to be the light that brings truth and brings hope.

Isaiah 9:2 – *"The people who walked in darkness have seen a great light."*

When Jesus was born, light broke through centuries of silence and despair. The shepherds in the field saw the glory of God shine round them. The Magi followed a star, a symbol that heaven's light had entered the earth. Jesus didn't just bring light; **He is the light.**

Luke 2:9–11 – *"The glory of the Lord shone round about them... For unto you is born this day a Savior."*

Herod tried to kill Him. The world tried to silence Him. Even death tried to hold Him, but the light could not be overcome! Evil, hatred, and unbelief have always opposed the light of Christ, yet they can never extinguish it. The empty tomb proves that darkness never wins.

John 3:19–20 – *"Light has come into the world, but people loved darkness instead of light."*

Jesus came to shine His light in us and through us. We are called to reflect His brightness in a dark and hurting world. Every act of kindness, every word of truth, and every expression of love is a spark of His light shining through us.
Philippians 2:15 – *"Shine like stars in the world."*

The story of Christmas points us toward eternity—a future where darkness will be no more. The light that began in Bethlehem will one day fill the whole world. In heaven, there will be no night, no tears, and no shadows, only eternal light of the Lamb.
Revelation 22:5 – *"They need no lamp or sun, for the Lord God will be their light."*

Christmas is God's declaration that **light is stronger than darkness, hope is stronger than despair, and love is stronger than fear.** When we celebrate Jesus' birth, we celebrate the light that still shines—in our hearts, our homes, and our world.

Reflection Questions:

- In what ways do you see "spiritual darkness" in our world today?
- What does it mean to you personally that Jesus is "the light of the world"?
- When have you felt like darkness was trying to overcome your light, and how did God strengthen you?
- How can you be the light of Jesus shining through your life this Christmas?
- How does the promise of eternal light give you hope during dark or difficult times?

Prayer:
"Lord Jesus, thank You for being the light that shines in our darkness. Help us walk in Your light, to reflect Your love, and to share Your hope with others this

Christmas season. Amen."

December 21 – The Waiting Ends

Adapted from a sermon by Pastor Aaron Routon

"When the time came to completion, God sent his Son, born of a woman, born under the law, to redeem those under the law, so that we might receive adoption as sons." - Galatians 4:4–5 (CSB)

Reflection:

From the moment Adam and Eve sinned, God spoke to the serpent and said, "He shall bruise your head and you will bruise his heel." Even then, there was a promise—one day the fight between man and evil would come to an end. Throughout the years, God's people endured wars, pain, and waiting, hoping for a King who would bring an end to suffering and finally make things right.

God always answers. To Moses He said, "I will raise up for them a prophet like you from among their brothers." It was a word of hope—a promise that someone greater was coming. And for over six hundred years, God's people held onto that word, trusting it through every season of silence and struggle.

Then came the words of Isaiah, the prophet who spoke more hope than any other about the coming Messiah: "Therefore the Lord himself will give you a sign: behold, the virgin shall conceive and bear a son, and shall call his name Immanuel." "For unto us a child is born, a son is given, and his name will be called Wonderful Counselor, Mighty God, Everlasting Father, Prince of Peace." "He was pierced for our transgressions, and with his wounds we are healed." Those words carried light for generations—and they still do today.

But then came silence. Complete silence. The word of the Lord ceased, and Scripture tells us there were four hundred years when no new revelation came. All the promises, all the hope—they seemed to stop. Yet even in the quiet, God was not absent. He had already spoken His Word, and His Word was alive. It never returns empty. Even when His people couldn't see it, God was still working, preparing the world for redemption.

And then—on one night in Bethlehem—Mary and Joseph arrived. In a simple stable, the King of Heaven was born. The hope that humanity had been waiting for finally appeared. Every word spoken by the prophets found its fulfillment in Him. His arrival changed history forever. Thirty-three years later, He would die on a cross, and that blood-stained cross would wash away our sin. It's only because of Jesus that hope is alive.

So today, hold on to that hope. Hold on to His Word. Hold on to His truth. John 1 reminds us, "In the beginning was the Word, and the Word became flesh and dwelt among us." That Word is alive and powerful. We have Jesus— but we also live among broken people and broken hearts who are still crying out for hope.

Will you share your song of hope this Christmas? Will you be the one who gives away the joy and peace that only Jesus can bring? There is still hope in Him. There is still a way out of the darkness, because Jesus is our hope.

Prayer:
Father, we come to You knowing that there is hope in Jesus' name. Help us to be the light that points to Jesus, the light of the world. Help us to share words of hope so others can see that You have delivered us and set us free. Let us be Your hands and feet so that lives are changed and people experience the hope of Jesus. In His mighty name, Amen.

December 22 – The True Meaning of Christmas

Adapted from a Bible study by Pastor William Reid

"But the angel said to them, 'Don't be afraid, for look, I proclaim to you good news of great joy that will be for all the people: Today in the city of David a Savior was born for you, who is the Messiah, the Lord.'" - Luke 2:10–11 (CSB)

Reflection:

Christmas is more than a holiday—it's the time we set apart to celebrate the birth of the Christ child. It's a time to celebrate the greatest gift that mankind has ever been given. Yet, every year, many people miss the true meaning of Christmas. Some become distracted, others indifferent, and some even hostile toward what it really represents.

But the wise men got it right. They said, *"We have seen His star in the east and have come to worship Him."* That's the heart of Christmas. That's where joy begins—when we come to worship the Lord Jesus Christ. Joy is found in the presence of the Savior, not in the rush of the season or the gifts under a tree.

The wise men traveled a long way, facing distance and discomfort, but their journey was filled with purpose. They weren't chasing tradition; they were chasing truth. And when they found Him, they bowed down and worshiped. They didn't just give treasures of gold, frankincense, and myrrh—they gave their hearts. Because the greatest gift in that house wasn't what they brought; it was who they met.

This Christmas, you may face obstacles, busyness, or burdens, but don't lose your joy. Take a moment to be still and worship. See His star again. Feel His presence again. Experience His peace again. The true joy of Christmas is found when we lift up Jesus Christ, exalt Him, and glorify Him in our hearts.

Prayer:

Father, thank You for sending Your Son, the Savior of the world. Help us not to lose sight of the real joy of Christmas—the joy of knowing You. Keep us from distraction and fill our homes with worship. May our hearts join the angels in saying, "Glory to God in the highest, and on earth peace, goodwill toward men." In Jesus' name, Amen.

December 23 - The Gift We Couldn't Earn

Adapted from a sermon by Pastor Greg Morris

"He did not even spare his own Son but gave him up for us all. How will he not also with him grant us everything?" Romans 8:32 (CSB)

"The real message of Christmas is not the gifts that we give to each other. Rather, it is a reminder of the gift that God has given to each of us. It is the only gift that truly keeps on giving." — Greg Laurie

Reflection:

When you begin to look at the family tree of Jesus, you recognize that during the time of Christ it wasn't a line of credit or accomplishments that established your identity—it was your lineage. And when we look at the family tree of Jesus, we find that it reflects all of humanity. It doesn't leave anyone out.

You find in the family tree of Jesus murderers, abusers, the powerless, the oppressed, those who have been marginalized, foreigners and outsiders. There are people who are deeply hurting. His family tree is a mess—much like yours, much like mine. Yet that's what's wonderful about the Christmas story: *God so loved the world.*

Jesus claims those who are wandering, wondering, weary, and worn out.

The heartbreaking family lineage of Jesus throws a lifeline to all of us with heartbroken families. Whatever kind of family you came from, that's the exact kind of family that Jesus came from—and the exact kind He came for.

God takes the sin of humanity and says, "I will make something good," and He brings and gives the gift of His Son. The most monstrous evil of history—the tree stands tall at Calvary—and Jesus gives His life for us. Though you may feel rejected this morning, you're cherished. *God so loved the world.*

Rahab's story in the Bible reminds us that God's grace shows up in the most unlikely places. She lived in Jericho — a city far from God — and she had a reputation that made her an outcast. Yet when she heard what God had done for Israel, something stirred inside her. She said, *"I know that the Lord your God has given you this land."*

Rahab was a godless woman with a godless past in a godless place, and yet she believed. That gives me hope during this Christmas season — that God can still reveal Himself in places like that. He's never limited. He reaches into broken homes, dark corners, and hurting hearts. He pursues the prodigal, those in darkness, those who are far off.

That scarlet cord Rahab hung from her window points straight to Calvary — where Jesus stretched out His arms wide to receive anyone willing to come to Him. The same God who rescued Rahab rescues us.

Christmas is proof that God steps into hopeless stories. When it feels like all is lost, He sends His Son. He blesses, strengthens, enables, helps, heals, and saves. The tree with the greatest gift isn't wrapped in lights or ornaments — it's the cross of Calvary. And the promise still stands: *If God gave His Son, how much more will He give us everything we need?*

Prayer:
Father God in heaven, we love You. We are grateful for Your Son Jesus, who came

to change us, heal us, and redeem us from our broken, messed-up past. Thank You for being the God who saves and restores. Help us to be a light in the world around us and share the message and love of Jesus everywhere we go. In His name we pray, Amen.

December 24 - The Longing Before The Light

by Pastor T.J. Smith

"Because of our God's merciful compassion, the dawn from on high will visit us to shine on those who live in darkness and the shadow of death, to guide our feet into the way of peace." - Luke 1:78-79 (CSB)

"O come, O come, Emmanuel,
And ransom captive Israel,
That mourns in lonely exile here,
Until the Son of God appear.
Rejoice! Rejoice! Emmanuel
Shall come to thee, O Israel."
— 12th-century Latin hymn

Reflection:

All through history, God's people waited in the dark. Prophets spoke of a coming light, a promise that God would not stay distant forever. Every generation held on to that hope: that one day, mercy would come near.

Zechariah's words in Luke 1 came just before Jesus was born. He looked at the brokenness around him and declared that the dawn was on its way. "The dawn from on high will visit us." That single phrase carries the heartbeat of Christmas. The darkness isn't final. The light is coming.

Christmas can be hard sometimes. It might bring back memories of old times and people we've lost. I love the season, but part of it hurts sometimes. You can sit by a tree, hear the music, and still feel a little empty inside. But that's exactly the kind of world Jesus came into. He came into our world that was hurting, waiting, and hoping for something more.

God didn't wait for everything to be perfect before sending His Son. He stepped right into the middle of the pain, the confusion, and the waiting. That's what makes His love different. He doesn't stand at a distance. He draws near to the brokenhearted.

So if this season feels heavy, you're not alone. The same God who made a promise to bring peace hasn't changed. His light still breaks through the darkness, even when it feels dim. Hope didn't end in Bethlehem, it began there.

Prayer:

Father, thank You for Your mercy that breaks into our darkness. On this Christmas Eve, help us wait with faith and peace in our hearts. Remind us that Your light still shines, and Your compassion still visits us. Let our hope rest in Jesus, the dawn from on high. Amen.

December 25 - God With Us

Adapted from a sermon by Pastor Greg Morris

"See, the virgin will become pregnant and give birth to a son, and they will name him Immanuel, which is translated 'God is with us.'" -Matthew 1:23

Reflection:

The bottom line of Christmas—the bottom line of our entire faith—is this simple and profound truth: **Jesus Christ didn't send a messenger. He became the message. He came to us.**

The God of the universe, the Creator of everything we see and don't see, chose to step into human history personally. The infinite God compressed Himself into human form and downloaded Himself into our reality. And He didn't do it like an ordinary download—He was the ultimate upgrade to human experience.

Imagine the scene. The throne of heaven, radiant and glorious beyond description. Angels crying, "Holy, holy, holy," without ceasing. The Son dwelling in perfect unity with the Father and the Spirit, surrounded by worship that never stopped. There's no pain there, no tears there, no limits there—only power and majesty and joy.

Then there's the choice. The Son rises from His throne and descends. He trades the songs of angels for the cry of a newborn. Omnipotence for infant helplessness. The throne of heaven for a feeding trough. He who needed nothing now knows hunger. He who spoke the stars into being now lies beneath them. The King of glory will have calloused hands and dusty feet.

That's the mystery we celebrate—God did not remain distant. He didn't send a representative. He didn't appear in a vision. He came Himself. Fully God. Fully human. **Immanuel—God with us.** Not just near us. Not just for us. *With us.* That's a beautiful word, isn't it? With. It's intimate. It means He's here. He's close.

When you read the Christmas story and Matthew writes, *"All this took place to fulfill what the Lord said through the prophet..."*—that a virgin will conceive and bear a Son—they shall call His name Immanuel—he's describing a promise that took over 700 years to fulfill. Seven centuries of waiting. Generation after generation holding on to the hope that God would remember His people. And He did.

He moved into our neighborhood. He pitched His tent right in the middle of our mess. He didn't demand the best room in the inn; He made His dwelling with us. He didn't visit as a tourist. He came to stay. He camped out with us. He shared space, time, and experience with us. That's what *with* means. And when Jesus came, He proved something eternal: **God is not too good for your mess.** He stepped into our weakness, into our humanity, into all the parts of life that are hard to walk through. He knows hunger and exhaustion, disappointment and pain. He knows what it's like to be human.

When you're sitting by a hospital bed, He's there. When you're lying awake wondering what's next, He's there. When you've failed and you think you've gone too far, He's still there. He's not watching from a distance; He's walking right beside you. That's what Christmas means. That's what *Immanuel* means.

God is with us. So whatever you're facing today—joy or sorrow, strength or weakness, clarity or confusion—remember this: Jesus didn't send help from far away.

He came Himself. He came for you.

Prayer:

Father, thank You for sending more than a message—you sent Yourself. Thank You for moving into our world, into our neighborhood, into our lives. When things feel distant, remind us that You are near. Let us live in the peace and the power of knowing that Immanuel has come—and He is still with us and living in us. In Jesus' name, amen.

Closing Thoughts

As we come to the end of this devotional, remember this: Christmas isn't simply a warm tradition or a comforting story. It is the announcement that the God who created all things has stepped into the world He made — not from a safe distance, not as an observer, but as a Savior who draws near.

The birth of Jesus tells us something we could never discover on our own. It tells us that the deepest hope of the human heart isn't something we achieve; it's Someone we receive. God doesn't wait for us to rise to Him. He descends to us. He comes into the ordinary, the broken, the overlooked places we would never expect Him to be, and He calls them His dwelling.

If that's true — and it is — then you can face whatever stands before you. Not because you are strong enough, but because God has bound Himself to you in Christ. The One who came in weakness now walks with you in strength. The One who entered the world in vulnerability now holds your life in unfailing love.

So as you go from here, carry this with you:

The light that broke into the darkness has not gone out. God is still with us.

The Savior who stepped into our world has promised never to step away.

May that truth steady you, renew you, and draw you deeper into the wonder of the One who came — and the One who is still with you.

For More Information

Thank you for taking this journey with us.

We pray these reflections have drawn you closer to Jesus and filled your season with hope.

To learn more about Parkway Church, our ministries, and how to get connected, visit **www.myparkwaycog.com**.

Made in the USA
Middletown, DE
03 December 2025

22016096R00045